Heart to Heart

Poems

Patty Ho 何世嫻

Heart to Heart: Poems by Patty Ho (何世嫻) reveals a gentle and passionate heart longing to give and receive love and seeking to understand where love goes when life ends. The key topics and moods are Love, Loneliness, Longing and Loss. A different tone is set when she seeks to view reality from the perspective of other souls.

Patty Ho has an intense interest in poetry, philosophy and music and this, her debut poetry collection, integrates treasured quotations and inspiration from famous poets, philosophers, lyricists and composers. Her poetry is stimulated by flowers, trees, stars, statues, pictures and people.

Although personal relations are central to this work, history and current affairs are also subjects.

Heart to Heart is stunningly illustrated with reproductions of original watercolours by the poet's sister, Annie Ho (何世琪).

Supported by

The Hong Kong Arts Development Council fully supports freedom of artistic expression. The views and opinions expressed in this project do not represent the stand of the Council.

Heart to Heart

Poems

Patty Ho 何世嫻

Proverse Hong Kong

Heart to Heart: Poems
by Patty Ho 何世嫻
Second paperback edition
ISBN: 978-988-8228-46-1
Published by Proverse Hong Kong, May 2016.
Copyright © Proverse Hong Kong, May 2016.
Web site: www.proversepublishing.com

~~~~

OTHER EDITIONS - EBOOK
Heart to Heart: Poems
by Patty Ho 何世嫻
24Reader Ebook edition, June 2010. ISBN 978-988-19320-6-8
Published by Proverse Hong Kong, June 2010.
Copyright © Proverse Hong Kong, June 2010.

~~~~

OTHER EDITIONS - PAPERBACK
Heart to Heart: Poems by Patty Ho 何世嫻
Paperback, 1st edition, March 2010. ISBN 978-988-17724-0-4
Copyright © Proverse Hong Kong, March 2010.
Published by Proverse Hong Kong.

Enquiries: Proverse Hong Kong, P.O. Box 259, Tung Chung Post Office, Lantau, NT, Hong Kong SAR.
E: proverse@netvigator.com   W: proversepublishing.com

Moral Rights: The right of Patty Ho to be identified as the author of this book has been asserted by her in accordance with the Copyright, Designs and Patents Act 1988. The right of Winston Ka-Sun Chu to be identified as the author of "Preface" has been asserted by him in accordance with the Copyright, Designs and Patents Act 1988.

Printed in Hong Kong by Artist Hong Kong Co.
Page design, copy-editing & proof-reading by Proverse Hong Kong.
Cover design by Proverse Hong Kong, Errol Patrick Hugh and Anonymous.
Back cover photograph by Anonymous.

Original artwork by Annie Ho (何世琪). Photographs by Patty Ho, Jose Lau and Simon Tu.
Permission to reproduce "La Phalène" by "Balthus" has been received from Réunion des musées nationaux Agence Photographique, Paris. © ADAGP.
Correspondence about photographic and artwork permissions may be directed to Proverse Hong Kong.

Proverse Hong Kong
British Library Cataloguing in Publication Data (1st print edition)
Ho, Patty.
Heart to heart : poems.
1. Interpersonal relations--Poetry.
I. Title II. Ho, Annie. III. Bickley, Gillian
821.9'2-dc22

ISBN-13: 9789881772404

All rights reserved. No part of this publication may be reproduced, stored in a retrieval system, or transmitted, in any form or by any means, electronic, mechanical, photocopying, recording or otherwise, without the prior written permission of the publisher. The book is sold subject to the condition that it shall not, by way of trade or otherwise, be lent, re-sold, hired out or otherwise circulated without the publisher's prior written consent in any form of binding or cover other than that in which it is published and without a similar condition including this condition being imposed on the subsequent owner or purchaser. Please contact Proverse Hong Kong in writing, to request any and all permissions (including but not restricted to republishing, inclusion in anthologies, translation, reading, performance and use as set pieces in examinations and festivals).

Preface

It is refreshing to read passionate poetry that comes straight from the heart of a talented poet written without pretence or embellishment. Anyone reading this outstanding collection of poems, *Heart To Heart*, will be impressed by the originality of thoughts, feelings and literary expressions of its writer, Ms Patty Ho.

The highest achievement in poetry must be to steal the reader's heart without the person knowing it or understanding why. Patty has achieved this by her simple, sincere and unpretentious style. She does not use difficult words or expressions, yet her poetry captivates the reader through easy to visualize imagery. She uses lucid metaphors like in the poem "It's Love I Know", where she wrote: "The first light from heaven kisses the veil of your dream" and, "a touching song pouring out all your stars".

Patty is in love with nature. It is everywhere in her poetry. She sensitively describes so many charming aspects of nature. She could with the turn of a phrase paint a vivid word-picture for the reader. The purpose of art, borrowing the words of Shakespeare from Hamlet, is "to hold a mirror up to nature". Patty's poetry has definitely shown this to her readers.

Patty is also in love with life. In her poem "To ... ", she poignantly asks:– "Across the canvas of life, what patterns have we drawn with our heart's brush?" In her "Poems for Charlotte", Patty describes her tender feelings for her "little peach" daughter whom she kisses three times each day. The reader could identify with her and feel the motherly love she so movingly describes.

A great challenge in writing poetry is that it must be good and original and be able to convey deep emotions, subtle ideas and beautiful images. It is accomplished through the choice of the right words, the apt combination of expressions, the innovative association of ideas, etc. To achieve this by the simple style that Patty has adopted requires genuine talent and great effort because "the best of art is what seems no art".

Poetry is not a work of the intellect but of the heart. Patty has a tender poetic soul and is endowed with both the courage and the ability to describe her innermost feelings. In her poetry, she opens her heart and soul to us. Through her work, Patty enables her readers to feel what she felt and to see the beauty of nature that she had seen through her mind's eye. It is this exceptional talent that enables her to translate these feelings and images into highly readable poetry and which makes her an outstanding poet.

Patty's poetry is easy to enjoy. She writes in free verse which has the advantage that she seems to be speaking directly to her readers without the constraint and pretension of rhyme and rhythm. Free verse, without such discipline, is extremely difficult to write, but Patty has succeeded marvellously in her present work. The reader is invited to explore the richness of her poetry by savouring her poems one by one and thereby embark upon a very enjoyable emotional journey as I have done.

Patty's winning the endorsement of the Hong Kong Arts Development Council for the publication of this volume of poetry is richly deserved. I sincerely hope that her present book, *Heart To Heart*, will stimulate the interest of the Hong Kong community in poetry, especially amongst the younger generation.

Finally, I wish to thank Patty for giving me the honour and privilege of writing this preface to her book and for my great pleasure of reading this volume of her poetry which merits every success.

Winston Ka-Sun Chu
January 2010
Hong Kong

Author's Preface and Acknowledgements

This book is a collection of the poems that I have written mostly in the past five years. "All beings are like scattered coins, love is the string (which binds them together)".[1] If there is anything which links the poems in this book, it must be *love*. Here I mean love in a wide sense, which includes love between men and women, love between family members, love between friends, love of life and nature, love of poetry and beauty . . .. According to the philosopher Max Scheler, man is an *"ens amans"*[2], a being who loves; I hope that through this book I can share my beloved poetry with every *"ens amans"*.

    I would like to thank all who have inspired, encouraged or commented on my poetry writing. I also wish to express my gratitude to my sister Annie who kindly drew the pictures and my friends who provided the photographs for some of the poems, and special thanks to Gillian Bickley who kindly assisted me in publishing this book. If I were asked to say more about my poetry, I would only write:

It is homesickness,
a longing for home
where feelings warm and true,
with no need to disguise,
freely flow.

It is melancholy
of the silent petals
falling from the heart
when the wind blows
into a fading dream.

It is music
of a singing soul,
in which words dance
across the lonely distance
from heart to heart . . .

Patty Ho 何世嫻

Photographic and Artwork Permissions and Acknowledgements

Permission to reproduce the photograph of the original artwork, "La Phalène" (1959-1960) (AM1985-516) by Klossowski de Rola Balthasar (1908-2001) called "Balthus", has been received from Réunion des musées nationaux Agence Photographique, Paris. © ADAGP. Place: Paris, musée national d'Art moderne – Centre Georges Pompidou. © Photo CNAC/MNAM, Dist. RMN / Jacques Faujour.

Permission to reproduce the following original watercolours by Annie Ho has kindly been given by the artist: "One good line", "The Waves", "Enchantment", "Poppies", "Into the unknown", "A Poem", "A dream in a chamber", "Amazing Web", "Fragments", "The Thought", "A loving smile", "Waltz in B-flat major: The Dance", "Romance: L'Amour", "Lavender Blue", "The swing", "From Cinderella", "Can you tell me?", "Blue Waves". (All the former are illustrations to poems of the same name.)

Permission to reproduce photographic illustrations for certain poems has kindly been given as follows. By Patty Ho ('Of clouds and love', 'Romance: L'Amour', 'Two Spring Poems', 'To part'). By Jeffery Howe, Fine Arts Department, Boston College ('The Thought'). By Jose Lau ('Dreaming Lily', 'It's love I know'). By Simon Tu ('Paths of life', 'Poems without words').

Every effort has been made to seek permission from and to acknowledge the copyright holders of all material not in the public domain. If any oversight has occurred, we offer our apologies and will make good the deficiency in any subsequent edition(s) if it is brought to our attention.

For permission to reproduce artwork by Annie Ho (all about 25.5cm x 17.5cm in size), photographic illustrations by Patty Ho, Jose Lau and Simon Tu, please contact Proverse Hong Kong.

The photographic illustrations to the poem, 'L'Amour' and the poem, 'The Thought' are of the sculpture, "Psyche revived by Love's Kiss" (1793) by Antonio Canova (1757-1822) in the Louvre Gallery, Paris; and of the sculpture, "The Thought" (1886) by Auguste Rodin (1840-1917) in the Musée d'Orsay, Paris, respectively.

Heart to Heart: Poems by Patty Ho 何世嫻

I Be ahead of all parting
1. One good line — 13
2. Loneliness . . . — 15
3. The Waves — 17
4. To . . . — 18
5. Here we sit — 19
6. Enchantment — 21
7. Poppies — 23
8. Into the unknown — 25
9. Answers — 26
10. Solitude — 27
11. Paths of life — 29
12. A Poem — 31
13. Poem of love — 32

II It's all I have to bring to-day
14. A dream in a chamber — 35
15. Amazing Web — 37
16. Fragments — 39
17. Poems without words — 41
18. Waiting — 42
19. Fireworks — 43
20. The Thought — 45
21. Tears — 46
22. The Heavenly Stars — 47
23. Inspiration — 48
24. Love shall survive — 49
25. La Phalène — 51
26. A loving smile — 53
27. The Flight — 54

III Music of Love
28. Prelude: When night curtains softly fall — 56
29. Étude: A blue umbrella — 57

30. Fantasia	58
31. Serenade	59
32. Nocturne	61
33. Waltz in B-flat major: The Dance	63
34. Romance: L'Amour	65
35. A duet	66
36. So blue	67
37. A beautiful picture	68
38. Till the end of time	69
39. Of clouds and love	70
IV Heart to heart	
40. Lavender Blue	73
41. Poems for Charlotte, 1. The swing	75
42. Poems for Charlotte, 2. My little peach	76
43. Poems for Charlotte, 3. The winter sunshine	77
44. From Cinderella	79
45. A star to miss	81
46. Can you tell me?	83
47. If only . . .	84
48. Those lovely white threads	85
49. The way he looks at the clouds	87
50. 夢蓮 – dreaming lily	89
51. It's love I know	91
52. Her last words	92
Two Spring Poems	
53. To Spring	95
54. A Bauhinia Dream	96
55. Miss you	97
56. To part	99
57. Blue Waves	101
58. Heart to heart	102

I Be ahead of all parting

"Be ahead of all parting, as though it already were behind you, like the winter that has just gone by. For among these winters there is one so endlessly winter that only by wintering through it all will your heart survive."
— *Rainer Maria Rilke*

One good line

The hardest poem to write
is one's own life.
Is it a clean white sheet
for us to compose as we like?
Or is it a form set
with predestined theme and length
and a limited choice of words?

Oh so many times
my words get lost,
leading me nowhere;
empty echoes, no one to share with.
In the depths of our souls,
we are all so alone.

May time help me learn
to smile at my fate
and set it to my music
though the only listener is me.
Before my ink runs dry,
Please let me write
At least one good line.

Heart to Heart: Poems by Patty Ho

Loneliness . . .

It is the silence of a sigh,
the echoes of footsteps,
as down memory lane you tread.
A deserted swing sways in the breeze,
sketching a dear face you miss.
In the air a blue mist hangs,
spreading an emptiness immense.

It is the sound of laughter,
the noise of chatting,
flooding a crowded room where you stay.
People utter words of a different world;
none know the language of your soul.
People gather round you so close,
but with the distance of an ocean wide.

It is the lightness of a poem,
the weight of a word,
falling silent on your lips.
The music in your heart plays alone
and your soul longs to drift
with the clouds, the wind, the waves. . . .

The Waves

The waves are coming,
drawn by a mystic mover.
A symphony they are playing
of being and nothing,
of time and eternity,
daring and beautiful.

Come what may;
Let's leap into their embrace
to unlearn and relearn
the art of true singing,
and rise above the tide
to write our poems on the stars.

To . . .

Across the canvas of life,
what patterns have we drawn
with our heart's brush?
Under the immense sky,
have any tiny sparks we made
warmed another's heart?

When wrinkles have adorned our faces
like broken railway tracks where memories wander,
will we be wiser, kinder, and understand life better?
When our eyes have grown dimmer,
will we see things clearer and further?

Will our souls feel light
when life's end is near?
Shall we learn from the wind
blowing on its lone journey
from time immemorial to time infinite?

When the wind has passed,
will the music of its poems
still sing in someone's dream?
One day when we are gone,
will the beauty of the pattern
imprinted by our love stay on?

Here we sit

Here we sit, side by side,
in this soon vanishing moment.
Let us take a photo of our shadows
while they still stay close together
and imprint it on our hearts forever.
Today is just a memory for tomorrow.

Let us burn our silent thoughts
under the scorching sun.
Oh it may hurt (like love does hurt),
skin cracks, sweat bursts.
Let them melt, let them evaporate—
our joy, our sorrow, our lies,
our sins, our pride, our desires.
Let them die away . . . into nothingness.

We shall feel so light;
a puff of wind may carry us away
and we shall pass
from the burning heat
into the cool shade
where all pain will fade.

Enchantment

*"For everything that's lovely is
But a brief, dreamy kind delight..."*
    — W.B. Yeats

Is it a gust of wind
or music from heaven
that sweeps through the tree?
Oh see how the leaves fall —
swirling, lingering, then letting go,
rising to eternal beauty...
like feelings flowing from a heart
when touched by the notes of love.

How can we grasp
these dancing dreams?
Will they vanish without trace
or in our hearts forever stay?

Who writes this poem
of ineffable enchantment,
moving with time's flight
across the autumnal page?

Poppies

In your soul, passion flows.

How you embrace life
with your blood-red heart,
opening wide your petals under the sky.
The world wakes on your face —
sweet innocence, wild passion,
love, pain, joy and sorrow.
Your heart sings, leaps and bleeds,
rising above your fleeting life.

In your shadow, death looms.

Lured by your narcotic spell,
so many lives have been lost.
For your opium an island fell,[3]
its fate and history forever changed.
But why should you be blamed
for the wars and follies of men?
You only live to love, to dream,
to dance in the meadows green.

Oh come what may,
sweet love, sweet death.

Into the unknown

It matters no more;
feelings come, feelings go.
See how the leaves grow
and the breeze blows.
We are two tiny drops
flowing in the immense ocean,
so close and so distant.
Trivial is our pain
amidst the miseries in this world.

On different paths we must now go,
not knowing if they may cross again.
Leaves will fall into our hearts,
bringing back smiles and tears.
Time will run forward and backward,
dreams and memories sweeping
through the corridors of our mind.

Oh let my gaze linger
on your face a moment longer;
see how our stars glitter,
their teardrops of sweet sorrow
falling . . . melting away the snow.
So we will drift and roam
in the maze of the waves
as our dreams set sail
into the unknown . . ..

Answers

What do we find
at the end of each quest?
Do we love more
the desire or the desired,
the dream or the real?

The deeper we search,
the more intricate it seems
and we may feel lost
in the enigma of life.

Will the path of our hearts lead
to enlightenment or disillusionment?
Can we outlive our pain and despair
and face adversity and absurdity
with a tranquil and elevated soul?

The stars are silent;
they disclose no answers.

Solitude

Be not afraid of solitude.
There are some moments, some feelings,
we must on our own face and bear;
and alone we must stand
before the door of death
when fate makes its final call.

Embrace the beauty of solitude.
In its serenity and silence
we may read the poems on the stars
and listen to the music of our souls;
memories fall softly like the snow.

It is in those solitary hours
that lovers truly feel
the depth of their love
reaching out to each other
across the lonely distance.

Paths of life

Have you ever wondered
if you had taken
the path not chosen?
Would it lead to a place where
the sky is higher,
the stars shine brighter
and the flowers of your dream bloom
beautiful and true?

Have you ever yearned
to ride on the wind of change?
Are you content to live
in the same way day after day?
Can the heart walk out
a new path from the old?

Between contemplation and action
where do you stand?
Do all paths lead
like veins of a leaf
eventually to the same end
where life breaks and falls?

Heart to Heart: Poems by Patty Ho

A Poem

No lovely green it wears,
all leaves are lost;
yet it stands firm and strong
under the cold wintry sky.

Without shame or reservation,
it holds out its sturdy branches,
laying bare its wounds,
offering its naked self like a poem
to embrace the immense heavens.

Around the empty branches hangs
a touching note of silence,
fearless of life and death.
Speechless and small I stand
Before such beauty and strength.

Poem of love

If death knocks at our door,
are we ready to go?
Are we willing to give up
everything we own, we love?

How could we bear to let go
of a dear hand we hold
that has warmed us, touched us,
in so many loving ways?
But who can make the choice
to go or to stay?

Perhaps our souls will meet
in the other world,
like two angelic stars
beneath the smiling moon,
and continue our poem of love.

II It's all I have to bring to-day

"It's all I have to bring to-day,
  This, and my heart beside,
  This, and my heart, and all the fields,
  And all the meadows wide."
— *Emily Dickinson*

A dream in a chamber

To draw in verse a rose,
you have to study it
for hours or days;
by its side you stay,
following it with your eyes,
feeling it with your heart
and dreaming *you* are a rose.

As the petals slowly unfold,
a whirlpool of red waves
freely spreads and flows;
smiles within smiles
overlap and embrace.
Such order in randomness,
such looseness in harmony.
What passion stains them red?
What love holds them close?

Life blooms and withers;
a dream opens and closes,
but it will slumber on
in the innermost chamber
which the petals have closed;
a dream they'll forever hold
even when all else is gone.
No eyes may penetrate
the secret at the core,
for the heart has its thoughts
the mind may never know.[4]
A dream in a chamber,
A chamber in a dream...

Amazing Web

It holds my gaze;
I cannot but feel amazed —
such creativity and artistry
the little spider displays,
as she moves across the air,
spinning her web of threads,
delicate and intricate,
an aesthetic piece of work.

A dreamer and poetess she is,
writing her poem on the web.
Like a trapeze artist she freely falls
and then climbs up in the air again,
adding one more lovely line to her work.
No companion or applause she needs;
alone but happy she feels,
weaving and weaving her dreams.

How could a mind in a tiny head
work out such an amazing web?
Futile her work may seem —
a strong wind may blow it away;
but she will go on
and be lost in her happiness
to create and dream again.

Fragments

Summer, sunshine, shower;
through emerald shadows,
from dream to dream we wander.

Beaches, oceans, freedoms;
heart waves dancing and breaking.
Seashells to pick, secrets to keep;
footprints buried in the shifting sand.

Wild sleepless nights—
row a boat across the moon river,
collecting stars to fill our dreams;
desires burning . . . dissolving
in the tender darkness.

Green hearts hanging in the air
grow towards each other
and drift apart;
fragments of memories
falling, lingering and fading.

So softly, so lightly,
between remembrance and forgetting,
the summer passes by.

*See those water drops on the leaf,
like tears dropped into a heart;
that lantern with pale yellow light
standing so lonesome in the dusk;
oh the smiling faces of the sakura,⁵
lovely maidens in sweet bloom…*

Poems without words
To S.T.

Each photo he took
is a silent poem,
to feel and to ponder—
a poem with no words,
no beginning, no end,
but images and lots of room
for imagination and music to roam;
a poem where time has stood still
in an eternal dream.

Waiting

It is a heart hanging in mid air,
not too high, not too low.
It can't fly up high,
missing something by its side.
It won't fall down yet,
sustained by lingering memories,
glistening hopes and dreams,
sometimes bright, sometimes dim.

It is a song that has stopped
in the middle of its playing,
maybe short, maybe long.
Some notes it has missed or lost
and in the suspended silence,
it searches for
an echo from a distant valley,
callings from desert and ocean,
and more beautiful music to play on.

Fireworks

Spellbound I stay,
fascinated by the fireworks display
dancing across and igniting the night sky.
With each explosion they make,
the feelings in my heart burst wild,
as the sparkling flowers shot up high
bloom and spread before my eyes,
madly burning their transient lives
to brighten the world of dark.
Showers and showers of colourful sparks
cascade over the mystic black ocean,
then vanishing away without any trace.
Dazzled and overwhelmed I am
by the outburst of beauty and ecstasy
fleeting but enchanting,
a nevermore dream soon to be gone.
In the next moment the sky will resume
its blankness, darkness and loneliness
as if no sparks had ever crossed its heart.

The Thought[6]

Headstrong lady,
what are you musing?
Are you pondering
your life, love and vocation?
Oh how you must suffer —
your body locked in a marble block;
but your thoughts soar far and high
across the boundless ocean and sky
to pursue your dream of love and art,
offering you a momentary escape
from the chains of human bondage.

Is life ruled by an inescapable fate,
entangled in the threads of destiny
from which one may never break free?
Why did your lover fail you,
and in his shadow forever you roam?
To meet him, love him, leave him
and be heartbroken, you were doomed —
eventually to be driven,
to the abyss of insanity,
and be eternally locked
in the prison of life and love.

Tears

Many sad and lonely hours,
they've accompanied me to pass.
So familiar they are to me
as they start their silent journey
streaming from the corner of my eyes,
rolling down my cheeks,
past my lips . . . into my heart.

Oh I know so well —
their touch on my skin,
their flow, their pace
across my stained face,
ah their bitter taste.

When love is too heavy,
when the heart is so helpless,
how can they be held back?
They are truer than words.

Oh let them fall, let them fall —
crystalline pearls from the heart,
so beautiful they are,
moved by the touch of love.

The Heavenly Stars

Have I wandered so far
just for this beautiful encounter in the dark?
As I turn my gaze towards the night sky,
so many stars twinkle before my eyes,
greeting me with lovely smiles.
In a world of change and doubt,
they remain steadfast and true,
bestowing on earth their eternal light of love.

Have I waited so long
just for one blissful moment to shine?
Oh calm my restless soul
and lift my weary heart
away from all earthly cares and bonds
into the embrace of the heavenly stars.

From the shore I hear the waves
playing songs of life and death,
so distant and so near.
Softly I close my eyes
and see the heavenly stars
shining and smiling inside me.

Inspiration

None knows when it will come.
Then on a sleepless autumn night,
like soft moonbeams it falls,
scattering a cluster of glistening stars
on the lake of my heart,
breaking it into ripples of music
swirling round and round.

Dance with me, my muse,
across the Milky Way;
fill me with sweet melodies
and wild imaginings.
Let my heart vibrate at your touch
and sing out high and low
a song of life and love.

Love shall survive

Is it only in the darkest hours
that the brightest light shines?
Is it only when lives are crushed
that the noblest human nature rises?
Is it only at times of loss
that we know what matters most?

When the world falls and tumbles,
what makes those mothers
use their bodies as buffers
to save the lives of their children?
What drives those teachers
risking their own lives
to protect their students?

As they lay down their bodies
and sacrifice themselves for others,
I see above the ruins and rubble
the most beautiful souls rising
filled with love and compassion,
stronger than the hardest rocks,
outshining the absurdity of fate.
Earth may quake and shatter,
life may be futile and fragile,
but love shall survive.

"La Phalène" (1959-1960) (AM1985-516) by Klossowski de Rola Balthasar (1908-2001) called "Balthus". © ADAGP. Place: Paris, musée national d'Art moderne - Centre Georges Pompidou. © Photo CNAC/MNAM, Dist. RMN / Jacques Faujour.

La Phalène[7]

What lures the moth
to fly into the fire,
consuming itself in the flames?
What tempts the lady
to chase after the moth,
tiptoeing to pursue her dream,
forgetting her naked self?

See how beautifully
the light illuminates
her dream butterfly,
and her gentle body.
Is she the moth
or the moth her?
Oh don't they know —
the danger in store,
the fragility of beauty,
the brevity of things lovely?

What draws me to the painting
and holds my gaze at it?
Is it the romantic light,
the soft misty colour,
the dream-like vision?
Or is it the finding
of my own self
in the lady, in the moth?

Heart to Heart: Poems by Patty Ho

A loving smile[8]
To Professor T.W. Kwan

Who brings them so close,
Jupiter, Venus and the moon,
forming a smiling face
hanging bright in the wintry sky?

So after all the endless waiting,
the two stars now meet
over the moon of hope,
breaking the cold of the night.

Parting and meeting,
missing and joining,
aren't they the same
but different modes of loving?

See how they shine
above the beautiful smile,
the two starry tears,
one of hope, one of love.

The Flight

To prepare herself for the flight —
she has to acquire
the courage of a bird
to soar high on its own
and venture into the unknown;

She has to learn
the grace of the clouds
as they dance across the heavens
following the music of their dreams;

She has to study
the philosophy of the wind
to move in harmony with nature,
to fall and to rise again;

Last but not least,
she has to let go of
desires that weigh her down.
So light and free she will feel
as she spreads her wings . . . to fly . . ..

III Music of Love

"Music, when soft voices die,
 Vibrates in the memory . . .
 And so thy thoughts, when thou art gone,
 Love itself shall slumber on."
— *Percy Bysshe Shelley*

Prelude: When night curtains softly fall

Stars write poems in the sky,
moonlight writes poems on the lake,
the wind writes poems upon the willow,
dreams write poems below my pillow;
Oh my dear, why don't you come near
and write a poem on my lips?

Étude: A blue umbrella

The rain weaves and weaves
a web of soft blue dreams . . .

Holding the same blue umbrella,
we'll go walking in the rain together.
Forget what tomorrow will bring;
listen to the singing of the rain.

What a melodious song it is playing,
with the raindrops gently falling
on the treetops, the pavement, the road lamps,
spitting and splashing, here, there, everywhere.

There is nothing more pleasant
than listening to these sweet sounds from heaven
under the same blue umbrella
with your sweet gentle lover.

Fantasia

If I could run so wild
into that imaginary world
where darkness shines
and raindrops smile;
If I could play and grasp
that music of eternity
where a moment is forever
and dreams fade never —
I would open and close a poem,
and fold it in your heart
with the tear of a star.
Then softly I'd slip away —
without any sound, without any trace,
like the snow melting into spring.

Serenade

Colour my dream
with the brush of your love.
Paint a smile
on the face of my moon.
Gather stars
and moonbeams
to weave a necklace for me.

May our hearts sing:
with our different voices,
blended in harmony and rhythm.
Love me please
for love's sake;
don't ask what we may reap.
Let love be a journey,
a never-ending dream,
in search of beauty and harmony;
forever we will fly . . .

Heart to Heart: Poems by Patty Ho

Nocturne

The night is burning
a poem of darkness;
its flames are singing
a song of nothingness.

In vain I search
for the moon in the waters.
Dreams look so real,
yet always beyond my reach.

When thoughts are too heavy,
I will lay them down
on a bed of rose petals
you scatter into my dream.

When words are too weak,
I will fall silent
and surrender my heart
to the embrace of the dark.

Heart to Heart: Poems by Patty Ho

Waltz in B-flat major: The Dance

The music has begun;
why don't you take my hand
and lead me to the dance?
Let's spin round and round
by the side of the moonlit stream,
our shadows merging in one dream;
to love is to dance,
when two souls come close
and swirl in the music of love.

If love is not a lie
nor merely a dream,
promise me please,
by the light of the moonbeam,
that you will wait for me
at the end of the rainbow bridge,
holding a bouquet of poems
written with the stars of your heart.

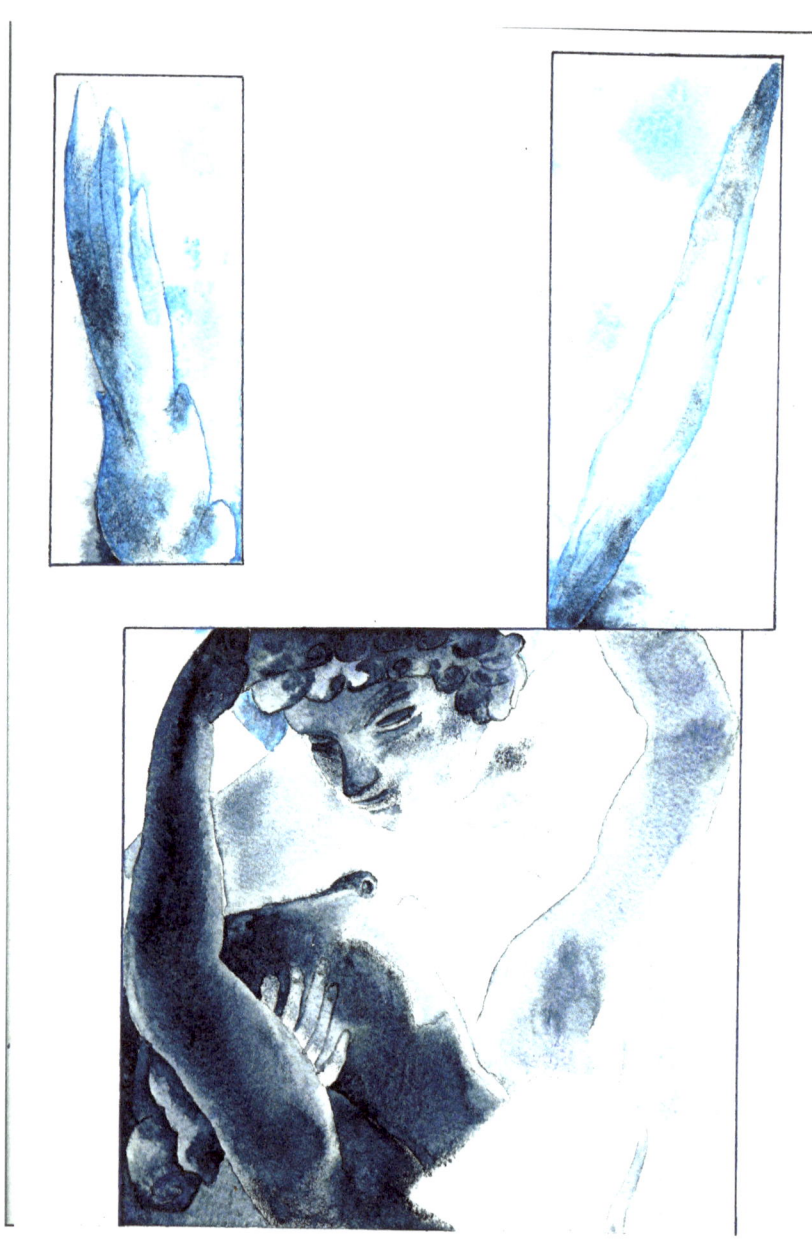

Heart to Heart: Poems by Patty Ho

Romance: L'Amour[9]

Come to me,
my angel dear.
Awake me please,
with your loving kiss.
Lift my burdened soul
and together we will fly
in the dreams of the clouds,
where being is light and free
and love true and pure.

Oh what mortal can withstand
the painful fall after the rise?
But never will I regret it;
feathers of memories will fall,
sorrowful and beautiful.
Nothing more shall I ask
once so high we soared
on the wings of love.

A duet

It isn't easy
to lay bare our feelings
and the wounds of our heart,
vulnerable to hurt.
Slowly we close our petals,
withdrawing into our inner selves
to preserve an unutterable beauty
and a moment of eternity.

From the initial sparks,
and the later yearning,
to the gradual waning,
we remain two solitudes,
still trying hard to learn
the art of holding on
and that of letting go.

Shall we see more clearly
by getting closer or further away?
Can we maintain a beautiful distance
without losing our intimacy?
Love isn't an easy duet to play
with the right tempo and touch;
it's a poem written by two hearts
upon a shooting star.

So blue

So blue, so blue,
the sky under which we stroll,
the dream in which we roam.
Blue is the language of our love.
My heart keeps drifting and drifting
in this boundless expanse of blue,
heading nowhere and everywhere.

Between dream and reality,
stillness and motion,
rising and falling,
desiring and touching,
lie freedom and limitation,
possibilities and impossibilities,
hopes and disillusion,
fullness and emptiness.

Perhaps there is nothing I care for more
than falling into your blue embrace,
the place where my dream begins,
the place where my dream ends.
Blue lights and shadows
dance, flicker and waver;
is this the beginning or the end?

A beautiful picture
To H.K.

I changed seats with him
to get a better view
of the young lady and her French lover
having dinner at the next table.
I understood not a word
for they conversed in French.
Yet her face was so expressive,
saying more than a thousand words,
and his eyes saw nothing
only her loving face,
spread before him, a rose in full bloom.
How she smiled at him
and how tenderly he gazed.
Sometimes his hands stretched out
across the table, searching her soft hands;
sometimes his fork lifted food
from his plate to put in her mouth.
Near the end of the dinner,
his body moved closer to hers
and hers slowly to his
until their lips met
and dissolved into a tender kiss
lingering so sweetly in the air.
I couldn't take my eyes off
this beautiful picture
which was much sweeter
than the dessert I had.

Till the end of time

「執子之手，與子偕老」[10]
"Holding your hand, to grow old with you"

It may just be an ordinary scene —
an old couple walking down a street;
yet there is something touching
that holds my gaze,
as the white threads on two heads
glisten in the cold morning air.

Each little step they take
seems such an effort to make,
but with resolve and grace,
in a slow adagio they move,
tenderly holding hands
for warmth and support.
Will they recall the moment
their hands first touched?

Their candles are burning low,
yet there is a beautiful glow
as solemnly with her he walks,
like in a scene he once did,
promising to hold her hand
and grow old with her … till the very end.

Of clouds and love
For L.F.

Are they dreams of the sky
spread like poems before our eyes,
or are they veils of illusions
that we may never pierce?
What lies on the other side
of the mirror of dreams?

See how they gather,
see how they part,
so graceful, so ethereal,
ever changing, ever drifting,
dancing with the wind of romance
in the music of silence.
Oh how they take my heart away . . .

Where do they come from
and where will they go,
sailing across the stage of blue?
Should we take love easy
as the wind blows,
as the clouds roam?
Is it only illusions we love?

IV Heart to heart

"Love one another, but make not a bond of love:
Let it rather be a moving sea between the shores of your souls."
— *Kahlil Gibran*

Lavender Blue
Dedicated to my dearest sister Annie

Lavender is beautiful
and so are memories
seen through the veil of love
in the mirror of nostalgia.

Each fading petal and leaf,
each loving word and smile,
I will collect
and spread them in my dream
to weave a cherished poem.

It isn't the number
of the days we live that counts,
but the loveliness of the patterns
a moment imprints in our hearts.

Oh lavender blue,
how you fill my days
with fragrance and sweetness
blended with a tint of sorrow
and a trace of melancholy.

Heart to Heart: Poems by Patty Ho

Poems for Charlotte

1. The swing

Come my little daughter,
let's go swinging together.
Up in the air we will fly
like two birds free and wild
till we reach a point so high
that we almost touch the sky.
Shall we give the clouds a loving kiss
and sing them a soft sweet song?

Rising and falling,
falling and rising —
isn't it a wonderful feeling,
especially with your little darling?
Life is like going on a swing —
sometimes we fall, sometimes we rise;
sometimes we laugh, sometimes we cry.

One day from me you will fly
to find your own rainbow and dream;
but remember, my little dear,
whether you are far or near,
how closely we once sat on the swing
and how happily our hearts did sing.

Poems for Charlotte

2. My little peach

How I love to kiss
my daughter's plump cheeks,
fresh as a peach from the tree,
so soft, so sweet.
At least three times each day,
I kiss and kiss my little peach
and sometimes even more
when she is jolly and cute.

The morning kiss is often a hurried kiss
for usually she gets up late
and rushes to catch the school bus.
The afternoon kiss is what I like best,
as I hug my chatty bird flying back home
with news and jokes and smells from school.

The goodnight kiss is the most peaceful kiss.
No matter how we've quarreled about this or that
or how naughty she has been, driving me mad,
at last she does quietly settle in her bed,
and this last kiss will softly soothe away
any unpleasant feelings of the day.

Poems for Charlotte

3. The winter sunshine

I love the winter sunshine
falling on my shoulder,
so warm and tender
like the touch of a mother.
It melts away the distance
between heart and heart.

I love the happy smile
spread on a child's face,
so carefree and lovely
like a sweet little dolly.
It makes me forget my worry
at least for a short while.

I love the sweet embrace
my daughter and I share,
so affectionate and intimate;
there is nothing more I want
as her body clings close to mine
and in my arms I hold
my joy, my pride, my love . . .

Heart to Heart: Poems by Patty Ho

From Cinderella

My dear Prince,
forgive me please,
in such a hurry I had to leave;
there's so much work to complete,
loads to bear, mess to clear . . .
Our chance encounter has been
the sweetest surprise of my life.
But can't you see
we live in such different worlds?
"And they lived happily ever after"
is just a lie in a fairy tale.
Living in a doll's house isn't my wish.

Forget me please;
but forget you I never will —
your face so handsome and young,
your touch so gentle and warm.
When you led me to the dance,
stars began to swirl round and round.
Never had I known before
how high a heart might soar.
If only the music would never stop
and we could go spinning on and on.
Yet I'm afraid —
lovely things can't forever stay;
love will fade and dreams fly away.

Let me vanish please;
all magic came to an end
at the final stroke of twelve.
I want to remember you
as when you last held me so close
with the light of love in your eyes

as if you would never let me go.
If forget me you can't,
take the glass slipper I left
and keep it as a fond memory
of the beautiful dream we shared.
Perhaps one day we will meet
if love is true, if love is deep.

A star to miss

If remembrance is a form of meeting,
we do not lack
bittersweet encounters
across the space of time;
on a dark horse we ride
towards a world of nowhere.

Each lonesome night
on the canvas of my heart,
I would portray an image,
assembling the scattered pieces
of a smile or gaze left behind.

Memories of love enrich our souls.
We need some tears to fall
to nourish and purify our hearts;
we need a star to miss
on a starless dreamless night.

Can you tell me?

Can you tell me —
how to measure the distance
between heart and heart?

Can you tell me —
where does the sea end
and the sky begin?

Can you tell me —
will a rainbow grow
when soul swirls with soul?

If only . . .

If only I could take down
a corner of this beautiful sky
and spread it before your eyes.
If only I could paint for you
a picture of this stretch of blue:
the sky bending down to kiss the sea,
the sea melting in the love of the sky,
all this grace and beauty
flowing so tenderly around.

Dusk is softly falling;
clouds are dreamingly sailing
across the velvet blue canvas,
brushing it with strokes
of pink, red, scarlet, purple . . .
changing, glowing, fading
with the last ray of light.
Soon darkness will creep in,
merging sea and sky, enfolding all.
If only I could fly across the night
into the nocturne of your dream.

Those lovely white threads

He bent down his body
to tie the shoelace of their sweetie.
Against the bright sunlight
she saw so many short white threads
glistening silently on his head.
How guilty she suddenly felt
as if she were the culprit
for turning them white
with all the worries she filled his mind.
How she wished to kiss them gently,
all those lovely white threads,
and sprinkle them with her foolish tears.

Heart to Heart: Poems by Patty Ho

The way he looks at the clouds

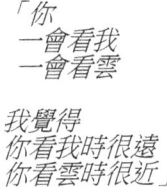

"You
Sometimes look at me
Sometimes at the clouds

I feel
You look at me very far
You look at the clouds very close"[11]

How these lines of a poem
touch something in her heart.
How remote she feels
when close to him she sits,
his eyes look past her,
gazing at the roaming clouds.
Her presence seems an absence,
a shadow in the distance.

Love is silent
when its music is lost.
She wants to buy a long white dress;
wearing it she may fly up to the sky
to join those lovely white clouds
so that he may look at her
more closely, more tenderly,
the way he looks at the clouds.

夢蓮 — Dreaming lily
To J.L.

What dream is dancing
under your closed petals,
embraced by the silence
of floating green hearts?

Are you hypnotized
by the mystic darkness,
the shadowy beauty,
enfolding the night?

Has a star by chance fallen
into your tender bosom?
What secrets slumber
in your inmost chamber?

A beauty you hold,
seen only with eyes closed.
A starry dream you preserve
that no world can disturb.

What fate awaits you
when the morn dawns?
Will love greet you
when you open your eyes?

It's love I know
To Professor C.F.Cheung

The first light from heaven
kisses the veil of your dream.
The soft mist fades;
one by one you unfold
the pink pages of your poem.

With such pure delight,
your being shines.
Earth and sky
meet in your smile.
What makes you bloom,
like a touching song,
pouring out all your stars?

Oh it's love I know,
which overflows your soul;
with it you paint your essence.
Life may be a contingency,[12]
but you make it
beautiful and true.

Her last words

In the Sichuan earthquake, one of the victims rescued from the piles of ruins was a little baby girl; when found she was lying in the arms of her dead mother who protected her from death and the baby was still sucking milk from her mother's breast.

Oh this infinite darkness,
such unbearable heaviness,
all the mud and debris
covering my baby and my body.
Will I never again see the sky
and my baby's sweet smile?
May God have mercy,
spare the life of my baby;
I can give mine as the price.

Oh baby, please don't cry;
soon your dad will come
and rescue us from this hell.
How I wish I could now
be held in his strong arms,
feel his loving kisses
on my withering lips,
hear him whisper to me
tender words of love,
and tell him for the last time
how much I love him.

Oh baby, please hold on;
cling close to my breast.
Take this milk,
the last I may give.
Grow up strong and healthy,
loving and compassionate.

Stand tall; never be crushed
by the harshness of fate.
Remember my love for you;
I shall always be by your side
embracing you with my love
now and forever . . .

Two Spring Poems

I To Spring

Beethoven's Violin Sonata No. 5 in F major, Op. 24.

Into my heart you leap,
filling it with music,
serene and melodic;
footsteps of Spring
waltz across my dream.
Closer and closer you come,
tugging at my heartstrings,
embracing my soul in yours.

Love and longing —
your singing arouses.
Oh yearning for what?
Eternal desires . . . transcendence . . ..
What is true happiness?
Who can grasp it,
light as a feather,[13]
tender as water?

Bauhinia[14] blooms with hopes renewed.
Lilies awake from snow-white dreams.
On nature's path heart wanders free.
Oh soar with the wind,
Spring is here.

Two Spring Poems

II A bauhinia dream

Under the bauhinia tree,
let us weave
a fragrant pink dream
with each petal that falls,
with each leaf that sighs.

Under the smiling moon,
let us sow
our bauhinia dream.
What will grow,
who knows?

Miss you

Miss you
like a bird misses the sky
blue,
like a hill misses the mist
white,
like a star misses the moon
silver.

Miss you
when I open my eyes.
Miss you
when I close my eyes.
Miss you
when the world can't tell me why
we must be so far apart.

Heart to Heart: Poems by Patty Ho

To part . . .
For M.L.

To part is a second meeting
more intense, more loving . . .
to gaze at a beloved face in the distance
with a longing of the heaviest lightness,
to continue on the backstage of the mind
a blue dream of moonrise tenderness,
to feel in the recesses of the heart
a closeness no distance can part.

Heart to Heart: Poems by Patty Ho

Blue Waves

Waves surround us,
playing the melody of the sea,
a melody of the world's oldest dream.
Tenderly, tenderly,
lips write poems on lips,
wordless, timeless…

Soul swirls with soul,
separate and united
in the changing ocean.
The last tears
dance in the blue waves.
If the moon forgets to wake up,
it must be drunk in our closed eyes.

Heart to heart
To Anna

I often wonder
which is longer —
the distance between star and star
or heart and heart.
No map may show;
in darkness dreams roam.

How many miles have I to travel,
how many winters have I to pass,
before I reach at last
the doorstep of your heart?
The longest route I'll take,
not any shortcut.

I have got no key
to unlock the door.
Will the stone flower
when the snow melts?
May love be the password
to enter your heart.

About the author
Patty Ho (何世嫺) was born in Hong Kong. She studied law in the University of Hong Kong and is now practising as a solicitor in a local law firm. She is also at present studying philosophy under the Master of Arts in Philosophy (part-time) programme in the Chinese University of Hong Kong. Apart from being a law practitioner and a philosophy student, she has always been a poetry lover and poetry still remains what she loves most. She first started to write poems in Form Six in her secondary school days and since then she has kept up her interest in reading and writing poems. Time and experiences in life have deepened her love for poetry. What she strives to attain is to be like the lily in, 'It's love I know' – to unfold the pages of her poems, pour out her stars, and paint her own essence with love.

About the illustrator
Annie Ho (何世琪) was born in Hong Kong and educated in Hong Kong until she completed her O-level studies. She then went to study in England, undertook her undergraduate degree in Cambridge and later her post-graduate degree in Oxford. She is qualified as a social worker and has been working in the profession for over twenty years. She studied Fine Art as a mature student and majors in watercolour paintings. She has had three successful exhibitions and has taken on individual commissions. Her artwork includes landscapes as well as more abstract expressions of her Christian faith. Her exhibitions to date have offered experiences of image, music and words; inspiration for the paintings has come from traditional as well as contemporary religious music and writings. The images are colourful and imaginative. She also works on a voluntary basis as a Spiritual Director for the Church of England and seeks to enable others to make the link between art and spirituality.

Notes

[1] The original Chinese text is: < 萬物如散錢，一情為線索 >, from the preface to "Qing Shi" (情史) by Feng Menglong (馮夢龍).

[2] Max Scheler, *Selected Philosophical Essays*, translated by D.R. Lachterman (Northwesten University Press Evanston, 1973), pp. 110-111.

[3] Hong Kong was ceded by China to Britain in the Opium Wars of 1839-1842 and 1856-1860. (The New Territories were leased by China to Britain in 1898 for a period of ninety-nine years.)

[4] Blaise Pascal: "The heart has its reasons which reason does not know."

[5] "Sakura": Japanese flowering cherry tree.

[6] A portrait made by Auguste Rodin of his beloved student, muse and lover, Camille Claude, who subsequently parted with Rodin, suffered from paranoia and was incarcerated for more than thirty years in the Montdevergues Asylum until her death.

[7] The Geometer Moth (La Phalène), a painting by Balthasar Klossowski de Rola (Balthus) 1908-2001, donation by André et Henriette Gomès (1985) to Centre Pompidou, Musée National d'Art Moderne, Paris.

[8] On 1 December 2008, the crescent moon, Venus and Jupiter created a "smiling face", a triumvirate of the three brightest objects in the heavens, which may not be seen again for another forty years.

[9] The sculpture "Psyche revived by Love's Kiss" (1793) by Antonio Canova (1757-1822) in the Louvre Gallery, Paris. It recreates the moment at which Psyche is woken up from her deathly slumber by the kiss of Eros. From the sky Eros sweeps to awaken Psyche who throws up her arms to receive Eros's kiss.

[10] 擊鼓《詩經・邶風》.

[11] 顧城:「遠和近」 (Gu Cheng: "Far and near")

[12] The idea of "contingency" was used by Sartre in his novel *Nausea* to describe Man's existence as an occurrence that could find no necessary meaning in itself.

[13] 福輕乎羽 (Zhuangzi 4).

[14] Bauhinia blakeana is the floral emblem for the city of Hong Kong.

WRITE TO US!

We are interested to read your comments on
Patty Ho's, *Heart to Heart: Poems*.
Write to our email address, info@proversepublishing.com,
giving us a few sentences
which you are willing for us to publish,
describing your response to this book.
If your comments are chosen to be included
in our E-Newsletter or website,
we will select another title published by Proverse
and send you a complimentary copy.
When you write to us, please include your name,
email address and correspondence address.
Unless you state otherwise, we will assume that we may cut
or edit your comments for publication.
We will use your initials to attribute your comments.

PROVERSE HONG KONG

Proverse Hong Kong, co-founded by Gillian and Verner Bickley, is based in Hong Kong with long-term and developing regional and international connections.

Verner Bickley has led cultural and educational centres, departments, institutions and projects in many parts of the world. Gillian Bickley has recently concluded a career as a University teacher of English Literature spanning four continents. Proverse Hong Kong draws on their combined academic, administrative and teaching experience as well as varied long-term participation in reading, research, writing, editing, indexing, reviewing, publishing and authorship.

Proverse has published novels, novellas, fictionalized autobiography and biography, non-fiction (including (auto-) biography, diaries, history, memoirs, sport, travel narratives), single-author poetry collections, children's, teens / young adult and academic books. Other interests include academic works in the humanities, social sciences, cultural studies, linguistics and education. Some Proverse books have accompanying audio texts. Some are translated into Chinese.

Proverse welcomes authors who have a story to tell, wisdom, perceptions or information to convey, a person they want to memorialize, a neglect they want to remedy, a record they want to correct, a strong interest that they want to share, skills they want to teach, and who consciously seek to make a contribution to society in an informative, interesting and well-written way.

Proverse works with texts by non-native-speaker writers of English as well as by native English-speaking writers.

The name, "Proverse", combines the words "prose" and "verse" and is pronounced accordingly.

There is an informative article on Proverse by Verner Bickley in the November 2011 number of the online literary magazine, Asian Cha, at: www.asiancha.com/content/view/1010/318/

THE PROVERSE PRIZE

The Proverse Prize, an annual international competition for an unpublished book-length work of fiction, non-fiction, or poetry, was established in January 2008. Unusually for a competition of this nature, it is open to all who are at least eighteen on the date they sign the entry form and without restriction of nationality, residence or citizenship.

The objectives of the Proverse Prize are: to encourage excellence and / or excellence and usefulness in publishable written work in the English Language, which can, in varying degrees, "delight and instruct".

Entries are invited from anywhere in the world. Semi-finalists to date include writers born or resident in Andorra, Australia, Canada, Germany, Hong Kong, New Zealand, Nigeria, Singapore, Taiwan, The Bahamas, the PRC, the United Arab Emirates, the United Kingdom, the USA.

Proverse Prize Winners whose books have already been published by Proverse Hong Kong are: Laura Solomon, Rebecca Jane Tomasis, Gillian Jones, David Diskin, Peter Gregoire, Sophronia Liu, Birgit Linder, James McCarthy, Celia Claase, Philip Chatting.

FOUNDERS: Verner Bickley and Gillian Bickley. To celebrate their lifelong love of words in all their forms as readers, writers, editors, academics, performers, and publishers.
HONORARY LEGAL ADVISOR: Mr Raymond T. L. Tse.
HONORARY ACCOUNTANT: Mr Neville Chow.

HONORARY JUDGES: Anonymous.
HONORARY ADVISORS: Bahamian poet Marion Bethel; UK translator, Margaret Clarke; UK linguist & lexicographer David Crystal; Canadian poet and academic, Jonathan Hart; Swedish linguist, Björn Jernudd; Hong Kong University Librarian, Peter Sidorko; Singapore poet and academic, Edwin Thumboo; Czech novelist & poet Olga Walló.
HONORARY UK AGENT AND DISTRIBUTOR: Christine Penney
HONORARY ADMINISTRATORS: Proverse Hong Kong

The Prize
1) Publication by Proverse Hong Kong, with
2) Cash prize of HKD10,000 (HKD7.80 = approx. US$1.00)

If there are two winners, they will share the cash prize and both will be published.

Supplementary publication grants may be made to selected other entrants for publication by Proverse Hong Kong.

Summary Terms and Conditions

Please refer to the year-specific Proverse Prize Entry Form & Terms & Conditions, which are uploaded, no later than 14 April each year, to the Proverse Hong Kong website: <www.proversepublishing.com>.

The free Proverse E-Newsletter includes ongoing information about the Proverse Prize. To be put on the E-Newsletter mailing-list, email: info@proversepublishing.com with your request.

Enquiries by email to <info@proversepublishing.com>.

The Editing Experience
Winners and Joint-Winners of the Proverse Prize as well as Winners of Supplementary Prizes work with a member of the Proverse Editorial Team to finalise their entered work for publication.

KEY DATES FOR THE AWARD OF THE PROVERSE PRIZE IN ANY YEAR (subject to confirmation in any year)

Receipt of Entry Fees/Forms begins	[Variable, no later than] 14 April - 31 May
Receipt of entered manuscripts begins	1 May - 30 June
Announcement of semi-finalists	August-September of the year of entry
Announcement of finalists	October-December of the year of entry
Announcement of winner/max two winners	March / April to November of the year that follows the year of entry
Cash award Made	At the same time as publication of the winning work(s)
Publication of winning book(s)	Within the period, beginning in November of the year that follows the year of entry

POETRY PUBLISHED BY PROVERSE

Following Patty Ho's "Heart to Heart", you may also enjoy the following poetry collections published by Proverse.

Chasing Light, by Patricia Glinton Meicholas. November 2013.

China Suite and other Poems, by Gillian Bickley. November 2009.

For the Record and other Poems of Hong Kong, by Gillian Bickley. 2003.

Frida Kahlo's Cry and other Poems, by Laura Solomon, 2015.

Home, Away, Elsewhere, by Vaughan Rapatahana.

Immortelle and Bhandaaraa Poems, by Lelawattee Manoo-Rahming. 2011.

In Vitro, by Laura Solomon. 2nd ed. 2013.

Irreverent Poems for Pretentious People, by Henrik Hoeg, 2016.

Moving House and other Poems from Hong Kong, by Gillian Bickley. 2005.

Of Leaves & Ashes, by Patty Ho. 2016.

Of Symbols Misused by Mary-Jane Newton. March 2011.

Painting the Borrowed House: Poems, by Kate Rogers. 2008.

Perceptions, by Gillian Bickley. 2012.

Rain on the Pacific Coast, by Elbert Siu Ping Lee. 2013.

refrain, by Jason S. Polley. 2010.

Shadow Play, by James Norcliffe. 2012.

Shadows in Deferment, by Birgit Bunzel Linder. 2013.

Shifting Sands, by Deepa Vanjani. 2015.

Sightings: a collection of poetry, with an essay, 'Communicating Poems', by Gillian Bickley. 2007.

Smoked Pearl: Poems of Hong Kong and Beyond, by Akin Jeje (Akinsola Olufemi Jeje). 2010.

Unlocking, by Mary-Jane Newton. November 2013.

Wonder, Lust & Itchy Feet, by Sally Dellow. 2011.

POETRY – CHINESE LANGUAGE

For the Record and other Poems of Hong Kong, by Gillian Bickley. Translated into Chinese by Simon Chow. 2010. E-bk.

Moving House and other Poems from Hong Kong, translated into Chinese, with additional material, by Gillian Bickley. Edited by Tony Ming-Tak Yip. Translated by Tony Yip & others. 2008.

FIND OUT MORE ABOUT OUR AUTHORS BOOKS, EVENTS, AND THE PROVERSE PRIZE

Visit our website
http://www.proversepublishing.com

Visit our distributor's website
<www.chineseupress.com>

Follow us on Twitter
Follow news and conversation: <twitter.com/Proversebooks>
OR
Copy and paste the following to your browser window and follow the instructions: https://twitter.com/#!/ProverseBooks

"Like" us on www.facebook.com/ProversePress

Request our E-Newsletter
Send your request to info@proversepublishing.com.

Availability
Most titles are available in Hong Kong and world-wide from our Hong Kong based Distributor,
The Chinese University Press of Hong Kong,
The Chinese University of Hong Kong, Shatin, NT,
Hong Kong SAR, China. Web: chineseupress.com

All titles are available from Proverse Hong Kong and the Proverse Hong Kong UK-based Distributor.

We have stock-holding retailers in Hong Kong,
Singapore (Select Books),
Canada (Elizabeth Campbell Books),
Principality of Andorra (Llibreria La Puça, La Llibreria).
Orders can be made from bookshops in the UK and elsewhere.

Ebooks
Most of our titles are available also as Ebooks.

www.ingramcontent.com/pod-product-compliance
Lightning Source LLC
Chambersburg PA
CBHW042339150426
43195CB00006B/109